PLANTS vs. ZOMBIES™

SOIL YOUR PLANTS!

JOKE BOOK

PUFFIN

Contents

Hello You!   6
Food to Die For   8
Newspaper Zombie Loves Knock Knock Jokes   10
Braaains!   12
Fun-dead and Games   14
Mullet Zombie's Baddest Bad Gags   16
Aches and Paaains   18
Lookin' Good! (For a Zombie)   20
Chatterboxes   22
Flag Zombie Loves Colours (And Also Brains)   24
Odd Bods   26
Home and Garden   28
Future Zombie's Tech Talk   30
Wild West   32
Shop 'Til You Drop (Dead)   33
Food to Die For 2   34
Knock Knocking On Your Front Door   36
Zombie Yeti's Wildlife Jokes   38
Getting Around   40
Mullet Zombie's Extra Bad Gags   42

Aches and Paaains 2   44

Ancient Egypt   46

It's Gargantuar!   48

Dead Colourful   50

Odd Bods 2   52

Home and Garden 2   54

Party Time!   56

Love Is In the Air
(And So Is the Sound of Screaming)   58

Harsh Lessons   60

Food to Die For 3   62

Nighty Night   64

Hello You!

The end of the world is a real pain. There are zombies shuffling around everywhere, gardens are a mess and getting a pizza delivered is a write-off. How are you meant to enjoy yourself? It's rubbish!

So, to cheer you up, here's the first ever Plants vs. Zombies joke book. It's packed to the rafters with two distinct kinds of jokes:

Jokes about zombies, like these . . .

What does a polite zombie say after being introduced?
Pleased to eat you!

What is the best way to speak to an angry zombie?
From far away!

Why did the zombie comedian get booed off stage?
Because his jokes were rotten!

. . . and jokes about plants, like these . . .

Why didn't anyone laugh at Kernel-pult's jokes?
Because they were too corny!

What is the wobbliest plant?
A jelly bean!

What did the Potato Mine name his son?
Chip!

All you need to do is laugh! Oh, and read the jokes. And use your hands to hold the book and turn the pages. Does that all make sense so far? Yuppy yup? Nice! Then let's get on with it!

Food To Die For

Why did the zombie eat a light bulb?
He wanted a light snack!

How do zombies like their eggs?
Terror-fried!

Why don't zombies eat penguins?
Because they can't get the wrappers off!

What food do zombies fear most?
Peashooter soup!

What do zombies serve for dessert?
Ice SCREAM!

What two things can zombies not eat for breakfast?
Lunch and dinner!

What's a zombie's favourite kind of sausage?
A Hallo-wiener!

What does a zombie like to pour all over his dinner?
GRAVEy!

Newspaper Zombie Loves Knock Knock Jokes

Knock, knock!

Who's there?

Zombie.

Zombie who?

BRAAAAINSS!!

Knock, knock!

Who's there?

The interrupting zombie.

The interrupting zom . . .

BRAAAINNSS!!

Knock, knock!

Who's there?

Ice cream.

Ice cream who?

Ice cream because a zombie is coming!

Knock, knock!

Who's there?

Gonna eat.

Gonna eat who?

Gonna eat your braaainnss!!!

What do zombie construction workers use to reach high buildings?
Craaanes!

What does the zombie doctor cure?
Paaains!

What do vegetarian zombies eat?
Graaains!

Two zombies are shuffling along the road. The first zombie says, "Braaains!" The second zombie says, "That's what I was going to say!"

Fun-dead and Games

What did the zombie get a medal for?
Dead-ication!

Why did nobody win the annual zombie race?
It was a dead heat!

What is the fastest plant?
A runner bean!

What is a zombie's favourite game?
Musical scares!

Where did the zombie kick the football?
Into the ghoul!

Why did Cabbage-pult win the race?
Because it was ahead!

Mullet Zombie's Baddest Bad Gags

Who was the most famous zombie detective?
Sherlock Moans!

Why was the zombie caught speeding?
He left his foot on the accelerator!

What happened when the plant was questioned by the police?
It spilled the beans!

What do you call
a stolen spud?
A hot potato!

Why do potatoes
make excellent
detectives?
**Because they
keep their
eyes peeled!**

What does a zombie
say during a wrestling
match?
**Want a piece
of me?**

Aches and Paaains

What kind of zombie has the best hearing?
The eeriest!

Why are zombies green?
You'd be green too if you ate all those plants!

Did you hear about the zombie who lost his left arm and left leg?
He's all right now!

How do you make
an artichoke?
Strangle it!

What plant can
tie your stomach
in knots?
A string bean!

What did the grape do
when it got stepped on?
It let out a little wine!

How do you fix a
broken Pumpkin?
**With a pumpkin
patch!**

Lookin' GOOD!
(For a Zombie)

What do zombies use to style their hair?

Scarespray!

What type of make-up do zombie ladies wear?
Ma-SCARE-ra!

Why was the zombie missing a shoe?
Because he had one foot in the grave!

What jewels do zombies wear?
Tombstones!

What do you call a zombie with three eyes, four mouths and seven ears?
Ugly!

What do zombies wear when it's raining?
Braincoats!

Who won the zombie beauty contest?
No-BODY!

What kind of plant grows on your face?
Tulips!

How did the farmer fix his jeans?
With a cabbage patch!

21

Chatterboxes

What did the big Sunflower say to the little Sunflower?
What's up, bud?

What did the big tomato say to the little tomato who was lagging behind?
Ketchup!

What did Snow Pea say to the zombies?
Ice to meet you!

What did the zombie say when he couldn't understand a joke?
Could you repeater?

Two zombies are eating clown brains. One says to the other, **"Does this taste funny to you?"**

What's Imp short for?
Because he has little legs!

Flag Zombie Loves Colours
(And Also Brains)

What is small, red and whispers?
A hoarse radish!

Why did the tomato turn red?
Because it saw the salad dressing!

Why did the leaf go to the doctor?
He looked a little green!

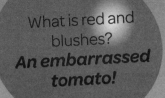

What is red and blushes?
An embarrassed tomato!

What's red and invisible?
No tomatoes!

What should you do with a blue zombie?
Try to cheer him up!

25

ODD BODS

What do you do if a zombie rolls his eyes at you? **Roll them back – he might need them!**

Why did the one-eyed zombie give up teaching? **Because he only had one pupil!**

What should you do if you see a zombie coming towards you? **Hope it's Halloween!**

Why was the zombie scared of heights? **Because he had no guts!**

Why shouldn't you tell a secret on a farm? **Potatoes have eyes, the corn has ears, and beanstalk!**

What kind of plant can fit on your hand? **A palm tree!**

What do you say to an unreasonable lettuce? **You should have your head examined!**

Home and Garden

Where do most zombies live?
On dead-end streets!

Why did the zombie put a 'keep out' sign in his garden?
To mark his terror-tory!

What is a zombie's favourite tree?
A ceme-tree!

What do you do if a zombie knocks on your door?
Don't answer it!

WELCOME

How can you tell if a tree is a dogwood? **By its bark!**

Why did the gardener plant light bulbs? **She wanted to grow a power plant!**

Why can't you iron a four-leaf clover? **Because you shouldn't press your luck!**

What has no fingers but many rings? **A tree!**

Future Zombie's Tech Talk

How do trees get on the Internet?
They log on!

How do you stop a zombie from biting his nails?
Replace the nails with screws!

What's a zombie's favourite type of movie?
A zom-com!

Why did the butterfly get a mobile phone? **She wanted to cauliflower!**

What do you call a super-fast fungus? **Mush-vroom!**

Why did the man get sacked from the banana factory? **Because he kept throwing away the bent ones!**

Why did Crazy Dave love his new hedge trimmer? **Because it was cutting-hedge technology!**

Wild West

Where did the zombie bite the Kernel-pult?
On the frontier!

Why did the bamboo get arrested?
He'd been in a shoot-out!

Why did Cowboy Zombie stand behind a horse?
He thought he might get a kick out of it!

What did Cowboy Zombie say to the horse?
Why the long face?

Why did Cactus cross the road?
Because he was stuck to the chicken!

PIRATES!

Harrrrr harrrrr!
Here be Pirate Zombie's
favourite pirate jokes!

What is the most dangerous plant to have on a pirate ship?
A leek!

Why did it take Pirate Zombie so long to learn the alphabet?
Because he'd spent years at sea (C)!

Why did Pirate Zombie make everyone stand at the back of the ship? **Because he was being very stern!**

Who cleans Pirate Zombie's bedroom? **A mer-maid!**

What did Pirate Zombie say to a man who insulted him? **I know you ARR, but what am AYE?**

Why didn't Pirate Zombie take a shower before walking the plank?
He knew he would wash up on shore later anyway!

What did Pirate Zombie say when his wooden leg got stuck in the freezer?
Shiver me timbers!

What does Pirate Zombie wear in the winter?
Long Johns!

What did Pirate Zombie say when he had a heart attack?
Arrr! Me heartie!

What kind of grades did Pirate Zombie get in school?
High seas!

How much did it cost Pirate Zombie to have his ears pierced?
A buck an ear!

When is Pirate Zombie like a bird?
When he's a-robbin'!

Why couldn't Pirate Zombie play cards?
He was standing on the deck!

What did the ocean say to Pirate Zombie?
Nothing, it just waved!

Why is Pirate Zombie so good at boxing?
Because he has a killer left hook!

How much did Pirate Zombie's treasure cost?
An arm and a leg!

What did Pirate Zombie say to the rock pool?
Show me your mussels!

Why did Pirate Zombie cross the sea?
To get to the other tide!

What do you get when you cross Pirate Zombie with a courgette?
A squashbuckler!

What did Pirate Zombie say as he walked the plank?
Water way to go!

Why are some zombies pirates?
They just arrrrrrr!

What was Pirate Zombie's favourite subject at school?
Arrrrrrrt!

What is Pirate Zombie's favourite sport?
Arrrrrchery!

What did Pirate Zombie say when Gargantuar stepped on his foot? **Arrrrrrrgh!**

What is Pirate Zombie's favourite type of music? **Arrrrr and B!**

Why did Pirate Zombie go to the cannon's party?
Because it was a blast!

What is Pirate Zombie always looking for, even though it's right behind him?
His booty!

How does Pirate Zombie travel around when he's not at sea?
In a carrrrr!

Where does Pirate Zombie order his drinks?
From the barrrrr!

How do Pirate Zombies talk to each other?
Aye to aye!

What is Pirate Zombie's favourite store?
The second hand shop!

What lies at the bottom of the ocean and twitches?
A nervous wreck!

When does Pirate Zombie buy a new ship?
When it's on sail!

What is Pirate Zombie's favourite letter of the alphabet?
Rrrr!

Why can't Pirate Zombie give up being a pirate?
Because he's hooked!

Why was Pirate Zombie made to walk the plank?
Because he didn't have a dog!

When does Pirate Zombie make a wish? **When he sees a shooting starrrrr!**

Who is Pirate Zombie's favourite fellow zombie? **Gargantu-arrrrr!**

Where does Pirate Zombie exercise? **Our gym, lad!**

How efficient is Pirate Zombie's ship? **Great – it does 60 miles to the galleon!**

Shop 'Til You Drop (Dead)

Why did the zombie cross the road?
To get to the second hand shop!

Where do zombies buy their food?
At the gross-ery store!

What did the tree do when the bank closed?
It started a new branch!

What do you call a zombie door-to-door salesman?
A dead ringer!

Where should you go when you want to buy a zombie?
The mon-store!

How are zombies able to spend so much money?
Because they're fun-dead!

Food to Die For 2

Why was the cucumber mad? **Because it was in a pickle!**

On what day do zombies eat brains?
Chewsday!
When is Chewsday?
Every day!

What do zombies call roller skaters?
Meals on wheels!

What do zombies like to spread on their bagels?
Scream cheese!

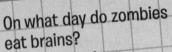

What did the zombie get when he was late for dinner?
The cold shoulder!

What kind of lettuce did they serve on the Titanic?
Iceberg!

Why did the zombie stare at the orange juice for four hours?
Because the carton said 'concentrate'!

With what vegetable can you throw away the outside, cook the inside, eat the outside and throw away the inside?
Corn!

Knock Knocking On Your Front Door

Knock, knock!

Who's there?

Amanda.

Amanda who?

Amanda-rin orange!

Knock, knock!

Who's there?

Ammonia.

Ammonia who?

Ammonia poor little Scaredy-shroom!

Knock, knock!

Who's there?

Lettuce.

Lettuce who?

Lettuce in and you'll see!

Knock, knock!

Who's there?

Turnip.

Turnip who?

Turnip the radio please!

Knock, knock!

Who's there?

Banana.

Banana who?

Knock, knock!

Who's there?

Banana.

Banana who?

Knock, knock!

Who's there?

Banana.

Banana who?

Knock, knock!

Who's there?

Orange.

Orange who?

Orange you glad I didn't say banana?

Knock, knock!

Who's there?

Bean.

Bean who?

Bean a while since I last saw ya!

Zombie Yeti's Wildlife Jokes

What is a frog's favourite flower?
A croak-us!

What is an elephant's favourite plant?
Squash!

What do you call an undead bumblebee?
A zom-bee!

What did the beaver say to the tree?
It's been nice gnawing you!

What kind of key can open a banana?
A monkey!

What do a flower and the letter 'A' have in common? **They both have a bee coming after them!**

What did the bee say to the flower? **Hi honey!**

Getting Around

What do Italian zombies eat?
Spook-ghetti!

Where is a zombie most likely to slip and fall?
Greece!

What do you call two rows of Cabbage-pults?
A dual cabbage way!

Where do zombies like to go swimming?
The Dead Sea!

Where else do zombies like to go swimming?
Lake Eerie!

Where do zombies like to go on cruises?
The Deaditerranean!

What's a zombie's favourite mode of transport?
A scare-o-plane!

Where can a zombie walk around aimlessly?
Rome!

BRAINS OR BUST

Mullet Zombie's Extra Bad Gags

Why did the zombie lose a lawsuit?
He didn't have a leg to stand on!

Why was Crazy Dave out of plants?
Because he hadn't botany!

What do you call an angry pea?
Grump-pea!

What did the plant lawyer say to the judge?
Iris my case!

Why did the pine tree get into trouble? **Because it was being knotty!**

Why are graveyards so noisy? **Because of all the coffin!**

How do you make a banana shake? **Creep up behind it and shout 'BOO!'**

Two peanuts are walking through a tough neighbourhood. **One of them is a salted!**

Aches and Paaains 2

Where does Sunflower go to the doctor?
The hos-petal!

Why did the zombie go to hospital?
He wanted to learn a few sick jokes!

What should a short-sighted zombie have?
Spooktacles!

Why did the banana go to the doctor? **Because it wasn't peeling well!**

What do you give to a sick lemon? *Lemon aid!*

What did the nut say when it sneezed? *Cashew!*

Ancient Egypt

What is Mummy Zombie's favourite music?
Wrap!

Why was Mummy Zombie so tense?
Because he was all wound up!

Why doesn't Mummy Zombie ever go on holiday?
He is afraid he will relax and unwind!

How does Mummy Zombie disguise himself?
He wears masking tape!

What did Mummy Zombie say to the detective?
Let's wrap this case up!

Why did Mummy Zombie call the doctor?
Because he was coffin!

Why couldn't Mummy Zombie answer the phone?
He was tied up!

Why would Mummy Zombie make an excellent spy?
Because he is good at keeping things under wraps!

IT'S GARGANTUAR!

What do you do if Gargantuar sits in front of you at the cinema?
Miss the film!

What is Gargantuar's favourite plant?
Squash!

What's big and ugly and goes up and down?
Gargantuar in a lift!

What time is it when Gargantuar sits on your garden fence?
Time to get a new fence!

Dead Colourful

What's red and green and wears boxing gloves?
Fruit punch!

What is square and yellow?
Sunflower in disguise!

What's grey and goes round and round?
A zombie stuck in a revolving door!

Why is a pea small and green? **If it was large and red it would be a fire engine!**

What's orange and sounds like a parrot? **A carrot!**

What did the zombie say after drinking a bottle of food colouring? **I feel like I've dyed a little inside!**

ODD BODS 2

Where do you find zombie snails?
At the end of zombie's fingers!

How many zombies make a stink?
A phew!

Why didn't the zombie go to the party?
Because he had no-body to go with!

Why do potatoes always argue?
Because they can never see eye to eye!

How do you stop a zombie from smelling?
Plug his nose!

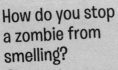

Why should you never tell secrets in a cornfield?
There are too many ears!

What is the strongest plant?
A muscle sprout!

Home and Garden 2

What room has no doors, no windows, no floor and no walls?
A mushroom!

What did Crazy Dave do when he lost his spade?
He hoped it would turnip!

What is a tree's least favourite month?
Sep-timber!

What did the zombies say about the neighbour's garden?
It really grows on you!

WELCOME

What runs around the garden without moving?
A fence!

What plant always grows in the basement?
Cellar-y!

What do you get if you cross a four-leaf clover with poison ivy?
A rash of good luck!

What is the safest room in your house during a zombie attack?
The living room!

What do you get if you cross a snowman with a zombie?
Frostbite!

PARTY TIME!

What is a zombie's favourite party game?
Hide and shriek!

Why do zombies go to weddings?
To toast the bride and groom!

Why are some zombies bad dancers?
They have two left feet!

Why do zombies dance so much?
Because they're fun-dead!

What did the tree wear
to the pool party?
Swimming trunks!

Why is Puff-shroom
always invited
to parties?
**Because he's
a fun guy!**

What's the difference
between a zombie and
a packet of crisps?
People like crisps!

Why are zombies
such good fun?
**Because they'll
leave you in
stitches!**

Why couldn't the
zombie hear after his
piano recital?
**Because he was
playing by ear!**

Love Is In the Air
(And So Is the Sound of Screaming)

Who does a zombie take out for dinner?
His ghoul-friend!

How did the zombie know his girlfriend was 'the one'?
It was love at first fright!

Where do plants like to go on dates?
The salad bar!

Why don't melons run away to get married?
Because they cantaloupe!

Harsh Lessons

How do you spell zombies backwards?
ZOMBIESBACKWARDS

What is a plant's favourite number?
Tree!

What's a zombie's favourite play?
Romeo and Ghouliet!

Why didn't the zombie pupils go to their lessons?
Because they were too ghoul for school!

What do you get if you divide Pumpkin's circumference by his diameter?
Pumpkin pi!

Why did the zombie want to learn about astrology?
He was interested in horror-scopes!

Why didn't the zombie go to school?
He felt rotten!

Why is a graveyard a great place to write a story?
There are so many plots there!

What did Imp's art teacher say about his latest drawing?
It's a monster-piece!

Why did the zombie buy a new gardening book?
He wanted to be a good weeder!

Food to Die For 3

Why do bananas
use suncream?
So they don't peel!

Why did the
jelly wobble?
**Because it
saw an apple
turnover!**

Which
vegetables go
best with jacket
potatoes?
**Button
mushrooms!**

How do you make a
zombie float?
**Take two scoops
of ice cream, a
glass of fizzy
pop and add one
zombie!**

What did the apple skin say to the apple? **I've got you covered!**

What did the lettuce say to the celery? **Quit stalking me!**

What do you call a retired plant? **A has-bean!**

What did the banana do when the zombie chased it? **Split!**

What is small, round and giggles a lot? **A tickled onion!**

NIGHTY NIGHT

Why did the zombie need a rest?
He was dead on his feet!

When do zombies go to sleep?
When they are dead tired!

Why are there fences around graveyards?
Because people are dying to get in!

What do zombies have at 11 o'clock every morning?
A coffin break!

What goes ha ha ha plonk?
A zombie laughing its head off!

What does it say on a zombie's tombstone?
Rest in pieces!